Change Your Thinking, Transform Your Life:

21 Truths to Renew Your Mind in Christ

By Michelle Stimpson

D1561844

Dedication

Christ Be Glorified!

Acknowledgments

Continually thanking God for the life-changing power of His Word. He's just good!

Thanks to my writing group for challenging me, sending me back to the Scriptures for clarification. Thanks for always reminding me of who I am in Christ, Lynne. And Patty, you *are* beautiful—inside and out!

Special thanks to fellow writer April Dishon Barker. You are such an encouragement to me! To my friend, Kim, for listening to these thoughts. Thanks, Donna, for the foreword. Your sweetness makes me smile.

Christal and Michelle, thanks so much for taking precious time to read during the holidays. Be blessed!

(From Paul's letter to the church at Colosse)

Colossians 2:8

Beware lest any man spoil you through philosophy and vain deceit, after the tradition of men, after the rudiments of the world, and not after Christ.

King James Version

See to it that no one takes you captive through hollow and deceptive philosophy, which depends on human tradition and the elemental spiritual forces of this world rather than on Christ.

New International Version

Don't let anyone capture you with empty philosophies and high-sounding nonsense that come from human thinking and from the spiritual powers of this world, rather than from Christ.

New Living Translation

See to it that no one carries you off as spoil *or* makes you yourselves captive by his so-called philosophy *and* intellectualism and vain deceit (idle fancies and plain nonsense), following human tradition (men's ideas of the material rather than the spiritual world), just crude notions following the rudimentary *and* elemental teachings of the universe and disregarding [the teachings of] Christ (the Messiah).

Amplified Bible

Table of Contents

Foreword

Michelle Stimpson, a woman after God's own heart with keen insight, has penned a challenging book for the believer to search and determine whether they're exercising common sense or uncommon sense in God's world. This book will draw you into a personal examination of how we think and act as believers. As Christians, are we being renewed in our minds as Christ commands us, or do we still delight in conforming to the world's way of thinking and responding? People are quick to say, "Common sense will tell you..."

This book will remind you that, as a believer, we're in this world, but not of the world. The Holy Scriptures and Scriptures alone guide our thinking, decisions, and actions. The Holy Spirit drives our responses. Scripture is used frequently to support the books content and points. Poignant questions are included to provoke serious answers from the believer according to God's Word.

This book is not only inspirational, it is illuminating. I am thankful for Michelle's clear style of expression and her love for Christ. Hopefully, when you read this book, you will walk away with (as I did) how awesome our God really is. His thinking and His ways are far above the world's perverted thinking. God is providing His people, through this book, with truths about the way believers are to be renewed in their minds daily. After all, "If anyone is in Christ, he is a new creation; the old has gone, the new has come" (2 Corinthians 5:17). Thanks, Michelle, for writing this delightful and timely book. Christ is truly glorified.

Donna A. Gantt-Founder/Author, Woman of Strength Ministry, Inc.

Introduction

As I sit here at the car dealership waiting to get my oil changed, the Holy Spirit just impressed upon me that I cannot run from this book anymore. I have to begin writing it. And I haven't wanted to write it because...well...here it is: I was not looking forward to the fact that this book would draw a line in the sand between mainstream Christians and me. Let alone humans and me.

But the irony in all of this is that the people of God are chosen and set apart from the world (1 Peter 2:9). We're not saved to think, reason, decide, give, live, or love like those who are not sanctified by God for His purposes.

While you and I may not look forward to the ostracism and rejection that is sure to accompany professing, practicing believers (John 15:18-25), we can rejoice in the fact that we are in good company. Christ was despised and rejected in His day, too— particularly by the more "learned," accomplished members of His society. They didn't appreciate the way He upturned the church's rules and taught people to believe in things that didn't make common sense (like the Messiah hailing from the town of Nazareth - John 1:46).

Yes, we are in good company. Excellent company.

Apostle Paul taught believers to forsake their cultural traditions and practices for this new life in Christ. Paul recognized that even though the new converts had believed on Christ as Savior, they were still influenced by their surroundings and worldly traditions. They still wanted to worship at the temple of Diana. They didn't recognize it as idol worship because it's what they'd always done. Common sense (the collection of knowledge that any given group of people holds to be truth outside and apart from the truth of God) cannot govern the life of a believer, whether living in Colosse or Colorado.

The point of this book is to expose current-day traditions and beliefs that don't line up with the Word. Resist the enemy's attempts to come and reason God's Word away. Where contradictions between man's way and God's way exist, let God be true and every man a liar.

The Spirit of God inside you knows the truth. He will not glorify the selfish, self-serving ways of man. He will only glorify the Son (John 16:14). As you encounter these truths daily, open yourself to His personalized teaching and receive the picture He paints of Himself in you.

In His Love,
Michelle Stimpson

Three Things You Have to Know Before You Read this Book

Some of this book cannot make sense to you if you are not a believer.

Let's define (by Scripture) what a believer is. A believer is someone who has confessed with their mouth and believed in their heart that Jesus is Lord (Romans 10:9). Walking down an aisle at church and saying some words that you don't actually believe does not make one a believer. Simply put, believers believe that Jesus is the full payment for sin.

If you are not yet a believer, there's good news—you're still breathing! The gospel is not reserved for people of certain backgrounds or nationalities. If you hear the whisper of the Holy Spirit within you, you have to know that the only reason you CAN hear His whisper or discern the yearning in your heart to come to God is because He is drawing you near (John 6:44). If that's YOU, do exactly what Romans 10:9 says. Confess Christ as Lord and believe in your heart that God raised Him from the dead. You are forgiven and saved from the power of sin. I am honored that God is using this book as a steppingstone in your eternal walk with Him.

If you are not a believer in Christ, much of this book will be a bunch of nonsense to you (1 Corinthians 2:14). I mean no disrespect to the people who ascribe to other gods. But the gospel of Christ is so uniquely based on His death, burial, and resurrection that I cannot assure you your god agrees.

Assume that the Bible is all true, even if you don't yet understand it.

If the part about salvation is true, then the part about heaven also has to be true. If the part about Lazarus is true, then the part about the talking donkey is also true. If the part about Adam and Eve is true, then the part about being submissive to your spouse is true. Granted, there arc times when there seem to be contradictions. There's the law in the Old Testament, but grace in the New Testament. Uzza died for touching the ark (1 Chronicles 13:9-10), but David didn't die for sleeping with a married woman and having her husband killed (2 Samuel 11). Paul persecuted the saints (Acts 8), but got to write a whole buncha books in the Bible—how did that happen?

I make no attempt to answer all of your questions. The beauty of Bible study is that it is full of endless revelation. If you have a question, ask God to show you the answer. Believe that He can and will at some time. (Believers believe, remember?)

As a believer, the ways of the world don't work well for you anymore.

13

God has committed Himself to transforming you into the image of Christ (Romans 8:29). Did you read that correctly? Yes, He has *committed* Himself to you, which means He will never give up on your transformation. Whatever God commits Himself to doing, He does. He cannot lie. Sometimes, the only question is if we're going to undergo this transformation the easy way or the hard way. Take my advice: It's easier to surrender your will to His and keep it moving already.

The things He does in you are meant to make you just like Christ—selfless, full of love, forgiving, ever-magnifying our Holy Father. Whatever you do, whatever challenges or joys you encounter in your marriage, your career, your family—all of it is part of a set-up to make you just like your Big Brother.

Which begs the question: why can't you just be YOU? Answer: because you're dead. The old you is dead. (Colossians 3:3). Let me try to explain.

When a loved one dies, you still know what that person would have said about a situation if they were here and how they would have reacted to a problem. You still have memories of that person. Sometimes, it may even seem as though you can feel them. You may be prompted to say and think things by their memory. But however hard it may be to accept, they are not here anymore and you will reach a point where you no longer make concessions for them.

It's hard at first. Shortly after my mother-in-law

passed away, I was doing my Christmas shopping. Out of routine, I actually took the time and effort to select the perfect Christmas gift for her. I made it all the way to the purchase counter, then suddenly remembered she was no longer with us. Saddened, I set the item aside and collected myself long enough to pay for the other gifts. A part of me wanted to buy it just because...I don't know...maybe if I bought it I could feel like she was still with us, like Christmas was going to be the same for our family. But I knew it wasn't reasonable for me to live as though she was still alive.

We all know that letting a loved one go (in your heart and in your actions) is paramount if you plan to move forward. Likewise, the old you died on the cross in Christ. You remember the hurts, the sins, the good times, the talents, the friends, your old way of thinking. But you must let the old you die if you plan to move forward in your life in Christ.

The good news is that the new you in Christ gets to live and function in this world as He did (1 John 4:17). This new you is better. All the talents, knowledge, and experiences you had as the old you are now submitted to God and will be used for His glory.

Be it unto you as you have believed.

1
Stop Thinking This:
You Deserve What You Get

The entire concept of what we "deserve" is predicated on the idea that our behavior determines our destiny. This philosophy helps people feel "safe" in an unpredictable world. If there's a way to connect the dots between what occurs in your life (good or bad) with something you've done, then you can control your life to a reasonable extent. The world loves to imagine itself as Master.

Additionally, people who are suffering can be judged by this myth because after all, if they'd done everything correctly, they wouldn't be suffering, right? By attributing people's successes or failures to what they've done or not, the world lulls itself into a false sense of security. But they *have* to believe this. If they don't, what hope or refuge would they have outside of themselves? What would save them from evil? How else could they "ensure" that they are okay?

Consider This

Some people call it karma, others say what goes around comes around. Still others base this philosophy on Galatians 6:7-8, which seems to support this false notion. However, the problem with this philosophy (for believers and unbelievers alike) is a little something called life.

Self-help and "spiritual" gurus would have you believe that you attracted or caused whatever happens. But none of them can explain what children do to "attract" abuse or why the drunk driver is the lone survivor of a deadly accident. And how can they explain why God sends rain on the just and the unjust alike (Matthew 5:44-45) outside of His love for us? More amazingly, what on earth did you or I ever do to attract or deserve God's goodness and grace?

So, what was God talking about when He said, "A man reaps what he sows"? In the context, God says that if you live a carnal life, you will receive what waits at the end of a carnal life—death. Contrarily, if you sow to spiritual things, you will reap spiritual reward. The road you choose to travel (by virtue of what you do with Christ) determines your eternal destination. The stops, twists, and loops along the road you choose are not indications of what you deserve. Ask Job! Ask Jesus!

Truth be told: If you and I got everything we deserved, we would both be dead. Sin requires the shedding of blood in order to be atoned for. Thank Jesus it was His blood and not yours.

Do yourself a favor. Stop measuring yourself (and everyone else) against the "deserving" stick. God has thrown that stick away. At the point when Jesus died on the cross 2,000 years ago, all of your sin was future tense. He has forgiven you for the sins you committed before you came to Him. How much more he forgives for those times you fall short afterward!

Learn from your mistakes but don't get caught up in this tit-for-tat system that the world uses to pacify its fears. You're a believer. Everything works for good in your life because you love Him (Romans 8:28).

Be Renewed in Your Mind

Job's friends tried to convince him that he must have done something wrong. How did Job respond to their accusations? How did God respond to their shenanigans? (Read the book of Job.)

John 9:1-7. What does this indicate about the "deserving" philosophy?

God is just, but is He fair? He's good, but is He nice?

Does God punish believers for sins that He forgave over 2,000 years ago?

Remember

God is not up in heaven keeping tally marks and doling out what you deserve based on your behavior. He has already overcompensated for your faults through Christ. Have more faith in His overwhelming

18

goodness than your ability to add to it or mess it up.

But I say unto you, Love your enemies, bless them that curse you, do good to them that hate you, and pray for them which despitefully use you, and persecute you; That ye may be the children of your Father which is in heaven: for he maketh his sun to rise on the evil and on the good, and sendeth rain on the just and on the unjust.
Matthew 5:44-45

And we know that all things work together for good to them that love God, to them who are the called according to his purpose.
Romans 8:28

Blessed is the man to whom the Lord will not impute sin.
Romans 4:8

2
Stop Thinking This:
You Can Be Anything You Want to Be

There is a great sense of hope in a country where just about anything can happen. One can be born in a county hospital and end up overseeing a major corporation. A person can become an overnight celebrity by posting a video online. If a person stays in school long enough and/or works hard enough, they can probably enjoy a prosperous life, particularly in the western world.

The world does its best to match skills and talents with desire and effort. But without the Creator's direction, occupation has no eternal value.

Aside from the spiritual aspect, it's amazing how many people preach this rule to young children, only to change their minds later and suggest safer, more predictable ventures. If the world really believed this rule, more of them would live it, especially since they don't have anyone to answer to.

Consider This

This rule isn't true for believers—not if we want to please God. Being *capable* of something and being *anointed* or *graced* to do something is not synonymous. As the opening line of Rick Warren's *The Purpose Driven Life* states, "It's not about you."

It is about Christ.

Believers must recognize that any opposition to this truth is straight from the enemy himself. It is our adversary who disguises his voice as your own and whispers, "I don't want to live my life for Jesus, I want to be normal and have fun! Plus, if I ask God what He wants me to do, He might tell me to do something I really don't want to do. That's gonna be a problem."

He's such a liar, liar, pants soon-to-be on fire!

Newsflash: God is good. The plan He has for you is good. And, according to Jesus, the best life you could ever have is the one He will give back to you once you surrender yours to Him (Matthew 16:25). The beauty of a life lived for Him is that as we grow spiritually, what we want and what God wants become one and the same.

The issue isn't necessarily what you *can* be, but what God has *designed* you to be. His grace, anointing, and authority are carried in the very Word He calls you. Besides, God is not obligated to bless plans He did not author.

Be Renewed in Your Mind

Has Matthew 6:33 been your experience? Has this been the experience of anyone you know?

Before you met Christ, what was your biggest fear about giving Him your life? Do you still have fears about surrendering to Him completely?

How can you tell the difference between a God-ordained opportunity and a distraction? A divine test and an attack from the enemy?

Remember

Live the dream God has been dreaming for you since He created you. It is better than anything you could think or imagine.

But seek ye first the kingdom of God, and his righteousness; and all these things shall be added unto you.
Matthew 6:33

For whosoever will save his life shall lose it: and whosoever will lose his life for my sake shall find it.
Matthew 16:25

3
Stop Thinking This:
Facts Rule

Facts and information drive the world's understanding. When an unbeliever comes face-to-face with facts, he or she has to make adjustments in light of those facts. If they don't they will surely be labeled as one "in denial" and suffer the consequences thereof. With no power higher than facts, there is no alternative for them.

Consider This

In Christ, there's a difference between the facts and the truth. Facts can be perceived by natural means—a checking account statement, an X-ray, the law. Facts are real, but they are subject to change. The terms facts, reality, and truth are not interchangeable. A lie is real, but it's not the truth. The truth, however, is the unchangeable Word of God (Mark 13:31).

One of the greatest examples of this truth is Abraham. Even after decades of childlessness, "Without weakening in his faith, he faced the fact that his body was as good as dead—since he was about a hundred years old—and that Sarah's womb was also dead." (Romans 4:19, NIV).

Abraham didn't deny the fact that he was old. Very old. Nor did he deny the fact that Sarah's womb hadn't functioned properly when she was young, let alone in these later years. Those were the real facts, folks.

And yet he believed because that's what believers do. We *believe* beyond what we see—the information, the facts, the currently perceived reality. We believe beyond the diagnosis, the certified letter, even our past experiences. Unlike the world, we serve a God who has decided to put us right in the middle of His glory through our relationship in Christ. He'd roll up the whole world like a paper napkin and throw it in the trash before one "tittle" of His word fails (Luke 16:17).

No. Believers don't grapple with the facts. We tackle and conquer contrary facts with faith in the Word!

Be Renewed in Your Mind

Have you ever seen facts changed by the power of the word of God? Have you ever actually believed the Word over facts?

How does the popular statement "It is what it is" breed hopelessness?

What's the difference between being "in denial" and

fighting the good fight of faith?

Read Romans 4:16-21.What's the difference between "calling those things that be not as though they were" (verse 17) and lying?

Remember

God's unchangeable truth supersedes temporal facts. Make the facts face the Word.

And it is easier for heaven and earth to pass, than one tittle of the law to fail.
Luke 16:17

Therefore it is of faith, that it might be by grace; to the end the promise might be sure to all the seed; not to that only which is of the law, but to that also which is of the faith of Abraham; who is the father of us all, (As it is written, I have made thee a father of many nations,) before him whom he believed, even God, who quickeneth the dead, and calleth those things which be not as though they were.
Romans 4:16-17

4
Stop Thinking This:
Education is the Key to Success

In the competitive world system, everyone is trying to gain an advantage by groping at something within his or her control. By pushing the notion that an education will level the playing ground for all and bring power, the world attempts to supply for the flesh through learning.

The very definition of success, of course, is greatly connected to monetary wealth in the world's system. Those with more education make more money, statistically speaking. Money, of course, allows one to appease the desires of the flesh and pride with things of this world. Put it all together and we get the world's idea: If you get an education, you will probably make more money (i.e., be successful) and be in a better position to control your life and get what you want.

Consider This

Controlling your life and getting what you want is absolutely not the goal for your life in Christ. God's ultimate objective for the believer's surrendered life is to conform you to the image of your Big Brother, Jesus (Romans 8:29). Education cannot be the key to the success God has in store for you because His purpose is bigger and beyond the reach of any institution-awarded certification or degree.

For a believer, an education may contribute to godly success when submitted to Him. Our Father may use education to develop discipline, put you in a place to meet your spouse, give you seed to sow, and/or position you to be a light in your profession (Daniel 1). In each circumstance, education is only a means to God's end.

On the flip side, God is able to teach, equip, and position people who do not have formal training. Since He is not bound by the world's system (i.e., pay your dues by going to school), He has the power to accelerate learning, bypass the rules, and set a believer up for success beyond those with more degrees than they can squeeze on a nameplate.

God's flair for upsetting the established "system" often creates panic for A-types and those who take pride in the idea that they earned their spots the hard way, by following all the rules and doing the right thing. What we all have to realize is that God cannot and will not be tamed by our self-serving constrictions. He is wild and wildly in love with His people.

Be Renewed in Your Mind

What temporal value is there in education? What about eternal value?

Can another person take an education or knowledge away from someone? By illness or accident?

What, if anything, does an education ensure?

What, if anything, is more important than education?

Remember

God makes planets. You hear me? *Planets!* His power and plans are not limited to man's simplistic formulas.

For whom he did foreknow, he also did predestinate to be conformed to the image of his Son, that he might be the firstborn among many brethren.
Romans 8:29

5
Stop Thinking This:
You Need High Self-Esteem

Without God's empowering Spirit, people of the world have nothing else to rely on except themselves. If they don't *feel* capable, they won't *be* capable because, again, they're all they've got. If people can somehow muster up enough self-esteem, they can appear to make life work for them. Yet, they live with a nagging suspicion that, one day, they'll be found out. Those who can't self-manufacture enough self-esteem are left to suffer their own self-fulfilling prophecies. The irony is that, in the end, everyone in the kingdom of darkness loses eternally.

Consider This

You don't have to look far in the Bible to find examples of people who didn't think they had what it took to do something great. Moses claimed to have a speech impediment that disqualified him from leadership (Exodus 4:10). Jeremiah thought he was too young to be a prophet (Jeremiah 1:6). Esther had everybody she knew fasting and praying for her because she wasn't sure she'd be able to pull off her big plan to save her people (Esther 4:16). I think it's pretty safe to say that self-esteem is not a requirement for believers.

God-esteem is.

Nowhere in Scripture are believers told to esteem ourselves capable of anything aside from what the power of God does within us. Philippians 4:13 says that we can do all things through Christ's strength. Christ never said "Have faith in yourself." He said, "Have faith in God." (Mark 11:22). Don't even have faith in your faith—have faith in The One who cannot fail. He called you and He is faithful to keep you (1 Thessalonians 5:23-24).

It is possible to accomplish an incredible feat without having a clue how God did it through you. You don't actually need to know how He does what He does. Be free of the expectation that you have to "feel" equipped or know exactly how to complete what the Lord tells you to do ahead of time. When God calls you something, the words He spoke actually carried the authority and grace to fulfill whatever He said.

When we rely on our strength, wisdom, self-esteem, He will allow us to experience the frustration of applying the world's rules to His system. Not a good match. In His kingdom, only Christ is glorified in us and through us.

Be Renewed in Your Mind

As a believer whose old self is dead in Christ, is it even possible for you to have self-esteem?

Read John 15. From His perspective, how much do we depend on Him?

Humor yourself: If self-esteem is something that is drawn from something deep within, how can a person "get" more of it from the outside world?

Remember

Your current ability is the ability of Christ, and His ability is limitless.

> *I can do all things through Christ which strengtheneth me.*
> Philippians 4:13

> *And Jesus answering saith unto them, Have faith in God.*
> Mark 11:22

> *And the very God of peace sanctify you wholly; and I pray God your whole spirit and soul and body be preserved blameless unto the coming of our Lord Jesus Christ. Faithful is he that calleth you, who also will do it.*
> 1 Thessalonians 5:23-24

6
Stop Thinking This:
You Need to Match the World's Description of Beauty

By having an ever-changing ideal standard of beauty, people of the world can quickly judge and esteem one another by external appearances. Earning an unfavorable judgment might lead to rejection in the professional or romantic realm. Thus, people put a great deal of emphasis on first impressions and how they present themselves to one another. They feel some part of their lives will be determined by how well they are received by other people.

For women, the stakes are perhaps higher. We will often endure painful, expensive procedures and time-consuming rituals to preserve the appearance of youth. This obsession serves at least three of the enemy's goals: 1) To keep people distracted by a never-ending quest for an unsustainable appearance; 2) To increase perversion. As the ideal female body becomes more child-like, the line between women and children is wickedly blurred; 3) To spur on a spirit of competition and comparison.

The quest for a certain ideal is built on a commonly held belief that the "better" you look, the more attention, adoration, and acceptance (i.e., love) you can expect to receive. Others who also play that worldly game further endorse this system.

Consider This

Mankind is beautiful by virtue of the fact that we are made in His image (Genesis 1:27). Step into a hypothetical scenario with me. I can't imagine God sitting in heaven telling the angels, "Well, we've made ten nice-looking ones. Time to make an ugly one now." Really? No. Not in His character. If anything, the angels marvel at each unique human God creates. It is only when the people get to earth that society tells us we're better or worse-looking than everyone else.

Contrary to popular belief, beauty is *not* in the eye of the beholder; it is in the eye of the Creator. He has fashioned every believer's appearance for His glory.

In recent years, perhaps as we've become a more global society, efforts have been made to embrace various shades and types of beauty. Yet, you can open any popular women's magazine and find a new diet plan or tips on making your "flaws" less noticeable. Who says your pear shape is a flaw? Who says your long nose is a flaw? Who says you'll get further quicker by looking like something or someone other than the amazing person God made you? Who is perpetuating all these lies?

The enemy of your soul. Don't listen to him. You are the best-looking you there will ever be, and no one can override God's plan for your life.

If people in your corner of the globe in this century happen to think you're beautiful, so be it. Leverage their misguided adoration to point toward His glory. If you happen to relocate to a country where you're suddenly deemed "ugly," so be it, too. Point them toward His glory anyway. Once they've fallen in love with your God, they can see the beauty of His glory in everything.

Be Renewed in Your Mind

Would the woman depicted in Leonardo's DaVinci's *Mona Lisa* painting still be considered beautiful today?

What do beauty standards say about a culture?

How does God see people (1 Samuel 16:7)? Can the Spirit of God teach you to do the same?

How can the pursuit or maintenance of beauty be a distraction?

Remember

God made carefully crafted every detail about everyone for His purposes. Who are we to disagree with Him?

So God created man in his own image, in the image of

God created he him; male and female created he them.
Genesis 1:27

He hath made every thing beautiful in his time: also he hath set the world in their heart, so that no man can find out the work that God maketh from the beginning to the end.
Ecclesiastes 3:11

I will praise thee; for I am fearfully and wonderfully made: marvellous are thy works; and that my soul knoweth right well.
Psalm 139:14

7
Stop Thinking This:
You Need More Money

The love of money is the root of all evil (1 Timothy 6:10). No matter how much money a person has, he or she always wants more. By increasing the perceived need for money, the enemy stimulates evil and chokes the world by its own desires.

Consider This

This may come as a surprise to some, but God has very little use for money. He was God before money was ever invented, and He doesn't need money to be God now. He has always provided for His people and He always will—regardless of the economic climate. His hand is much longer than government, salaries, and dividends.

I am reminded of one of my favorite lines from Rick Warren's book, "The Purpose Driven Life." The author asserts that you have all the time you need to do what you're supposed to be doing. If a believer is constantly pressed for time, we have to ask the Holy Spirit to show us where time is being wasted or misused.

The same is true for money. We have all the provision we need for what God has placed on our agendas (Philippians 4:19). To say that we lack what we need is to suggest that God has made a mistake; He has miscalculated and put us in a position beyond the scope of His provision. That has never happened. *Ever.*

While we may not currently posses the resources we need for tomorrow, next week, or next month, believers must recognize: We have everything we need when we need it. Tomorrow's "need" is not today's need and is not basis for accusing God of unfaithfulness. From God's hand to ours, we are abundantly supplied with everything we need pertaining to a righteous life in Christ (2 Peter 1:3). We lack nothing in Him.

Perhaps instead of focusing on the perceived need for more money, we would all do well to ask for greater revelation of wisdom and faith, and for a more productive use of the money, time, and talents we already have. Whatever we do with a little money is exactly what we would do with a lot of money (Luke 16:10). God is glorified when we honor Him with what we have where we are right now. Receive His provision in faith.

Be Renewed in Your Mind

Why would the enemy lie to us about God's provision?

If the Bible says one thing but your circumstances say

another, which one is real?

Read Matthew 6 and Philippians 4. How can you express yourself to God without accusing Him of neglecting you?

How do you currently honor God with what you already have?

Remember

God will take care of you for all eternity. You don't have to wait until you get to heaven to rest in His provision. As far as His loving provision is concerned, eternity has already begun for you.

Take therefore no thought for the morrow: for the morrow shall take thought for the things of itself. Sufficient unto the day is the evil thereof.
Matthew 6:34

According as his divine power hath given unto us all things that pertain unto life and godliness, through the knowledge of him that hath called us to glory and virtue: Whereby are given unto us exceeding great and precious promises: that by these ye might be partakers of the divine nature, having escaped the corruption that is in the world through lust.
2 Peter 1:3-4

8
Stop Thinking This:
Hard Work is the Key to Success

People like to think that if they work more, they can control what happens to them. And yet, the world's system actually discounts its own philosophy. We all know celebrated personalities who haven't actually done anything to become successful other than post a video on YouTube. Then, there are others (a great majority) who work 60+ hours a week and pour blood, sweat, and tears into something that isn't proportionally rewarding.

Those who do work hard and achieve the world's definition of success can attribute their state to themselves (or a team of other humans), or to "lucky breaks." Perhaps they will give God marginal credit, but the fruit of their success is pride.

Consider This

Life in Christ is not hard work. Jesus' appeal to us in Matthew 11:28 is to come and take up His yoke, which is easy. The load and the cross He asks us to bear are light in comparison to the burden of a life lived as a slave to sin. I submit to you that what makes the ups and downs of life even more difficult for a believer is when he or she tries to live the Christian life in their own strength, according to the world's ways. Life is actually *worse* for an independent believer because they can do nothing in the power of their old, dead selves (John 15:5). Trying to carry the world's cross and Christ's cross at the same time would wear anyone out! Pick the lighter cross.

The work we do accomplish is performed by power within. Believers who love to take credit for how long they labored in the word, how many hours they spent praying and fasting, etc., have forgotten that whatever they've managed to do was done by the power of God working within (Philippians 2:12-13). Humility dictates that whatever we know, we've been taught by Him so as not to brag, but to give God glory for the things He has done (2 Corinthians 11).

Godly success, both in this life and beyond, is guaranteed in Christ. If you received the capacity to believe that the Son of Man, whom you've never seen, died over 2000 years ago and will testify on your behalf at judgment, you also possess the capacity to believe Him for everything else between then and now. The work of this life is small peanuts compared to the supernatural miracle He's already done for us. Receive it. Work in it. Rest in it.

Be Renewed in Your Mind

In light of God's love for us, have we actually done anything we can be proud of?

Read the story of Jesus at the home of Mary and Martha (Luke 10:38-42). What's the difference between resting in Christ and being lazy?

How does God take care of people who can't work?

In your experience, which is harder—being of Christ or of the world? Examine your thoughts.

Remember

Character-training exercises (often disguised as "hard work") are a *part* of success, but Christ is the *key* to success for the believer.

I am the vine, ye are the branches: He that abideth in me, and I in him, the same bringeth forth much fruit: for without me ye can do nothing.
John 15:5

Wherefore, my beloved, as ye have always obeyed, not as in my presence only, but now much more in my absence, work out your own salvation with fear and trembling. For it is God which worketh in you both to will and to do of his good pleasure.
Philippians 2:12-13

9
Stop Thinking This:
Competing is a Way of Life

Competition is at the crux of our global economy. Businesses, television shows, even books are ranked in order to show which are "better" than others. We're a system set up for competition—from Nielson ratings to the valedictorians to employees of the month. While there's nothing wrong with recognizing people for a job well done, there's a difference between honoring and setting up a sense of competition.

Honor comes without comparison. Competition comes with stated winners and implied losers.

Consider This

Though believers may enjoy sports and other recreational contests, we must be diligent to draw the line where spiritual matters are concerned. There is no competition in Christ, and we're not competing with the world. Each of us is called to run the race that has been marked out for us (Hebrews 12:1). We run this race with everything He puts in us, keeping our eyes on the prize of Christ.

One of the cruelest aspects about the world's propensity to hold everyone to a measuring stick is that so few can win. No matter how hard you work, how determined you are, you win some and you lose some. At best, in the world's system, everyone who is disciplined enough will get the chance to compete at the highest level. People are honored, of course, to compete there. But still, only one can win the gold.

Kind of like a contest a local school district held. Every child who had perfect attendance for the school year had their names put into a big rolling ball. The superintendent then drew a name from the hundreds of kids who had qualified to be in the drawing, but only one won the prize. The others, though they had pressed through the year as much as the winner, did not get a reward.

God is not running a lottery here. His promises apply to all of His children, and He rewards those who seek Him (Hebrews 11:6). When believers mix the world's competitive reasoning with God's stay-in-your-lane-and-look-straight-ahead plan, we can be sure we have taken our eyes off Christ and fixed them on ourselves or some other idol. We can also be sure that we have lost sight of how faithful and wise our God is to the specific plan He has for us.

Be Renewed in Your Mind

Is there such a thing as "healthy" competition? If so, when does competition get "unhealthy"?

How does a misplaced sense of competition reveal

fear or insecurity?

Did Jesus ever compete with others?

Remember

Don't let the world's sense of competition infiltrate your motives. We have already won forever in Christ.

But without faith it is impossible to please him: for he that cometh to God must believe that he is, and that he is a rewarder of them that diligently seek him.
Hebrews 11:6

Wherefore seeing we also are compassed about with so great a cloud of witnesses, let us lay aside every weight, and the sin which doth so easily beset us, and let us run with patience the race that is set before us; Looking unto Jesus the author and finisher of our faith; who for the joy that was set before him endured the cross, despising the shame, and is set down at the right hand of the throne of God.
Hebrews 12:1-2

10
Stop Thinking Like This:
People Need Tough Love

People resort to tough love when they're tired of being used, abused, or made to look like an enabling fool. In such cases, tough love is used as a cover-up for unforgiveness, self-preservation, despair, and lack of wisdom.

Sometimes tough love appears to work by scaring people straight. Sometimes it doesn't, leaving broken hearts, relationships, and people in the aftermath. It's a gamble, but it's all the world has. The only other alternative is giving up.

Consider This

First, let's make sure we're on the same page about what my definition of "tough love": 1) sitting someone down and reading off their list of faults/problems; and/or 2) refusing to step in and help someone, which allows them to suffer the consequences of their choices. The hope in both instances is that the other person will learn from condemnation or suffering and quit making bad choices.

The delineation for believers isn't the "love" part—it's the "tough" part. And the issue is the heart. If we're doling out tough love in an effort to save face or protect our reputation, that's not love. That's fear.

And if we resort to tough love in a spirit of condemnation, manipulation, and ridicule, we're underestimating (and forgetting) the very love of God bestowed upon us while we were yet sinners (Romans 5:8). Tough love may lead a person to straighten up for a while, but Romans 2:4 tells us it's the goodness of God that leads man to repentance (the true heart change)—not Him forsaking us or His wrath.

The Bible does not describe love as "tough." In fact, 1 Corinthians 13 specifically says that love is patient and kind (NIV). Here's the thing about God: He can be patient, kind, forgiving, merciful, and every other descriptor in the Bible for very good reason. Aside from the truth that He's just downright good, He has nothing to lose! Christ has already paid the penalty for sin. God is free to love us without condemnation. If someone comes to Him one hundred times in a day and asks for forgiveness, what does it matter to Him? He might as well. I mean, He's already forgiven countless years' worth of stuff from trillions of people already, what reason would He have to stop now with us? He's not going to lose any money, time, or energy by forgiving trespasses. He can't lose face because in order to look foolish, He would need an audience of peers to make fun of His loving kindness. There is no such audience. No one is like Him, so He has no peers.

He's not scared of what might happen because

perfect love casts out fear (1 John 4:18). He can't run out of love because He is love (1 John 4:16). No one can *take* advantage of Him because He has *given* the advantage through His only son. He *expects* to forgive for the sake of love alone.

Here's the good thing about believers: We don't have anything to lose, either! We're already dead (Colossians 3:3). We have eternal life, everything works for good toward us because we love Him (Romans 8:28) and we have everything we need in Christ (2 Peter 1:3). We have absolutely no real reason to hold grudges, attempt to protect ourselves, fear, or be concerned with how others perceive our loving, restorative actions.

Receive wisdom from God on how to work through tough times in your relationships. Many of our conflicts can be resolved with an *extra* helping of gentle, loving-kindness, not less. There may come a time when you need to stop playing little-god so both you and your loved one can see God more clearly. Just remember that the goal is not to save the family name, the wallet, or to force people into a certain mold. Rather, we all desire to see Christ glorified.

There is actually nothing "tough" about allowing someone to fall into the capable, merciful, loving hands of God.

Be Renewed in Your Mind

Read the book of Jonah. How does God deal with Jonah's desire for the people of Nineveh to suffer in the last chapter?

How do fear and selfishness taint love?

How does God respond when we abuse His love?

What would happen if you loved people the way God loves them? Compare your thoughts with Matthew 5:1-12.

Remember

Our love for others cannot be "tougher" than God's love for us.

For if the service that condemns [the ministration of doom] had glory, how infinitely more abounding in splendor and glory must be the service that makes righteous [the ministry that produces and fosters righteous living and right standing with God]!
Corinthians 3:9 AMP

11
Stop Thinking This:
You Need to Vent to Other People

People feel the need to release anger, frustration, and complaints. Venting to others provide an opportunity to share life's disappointments with fellow humans who may be able to relate and sympathize. At best, one of the parties is wise enough to shift the focus from problem to solution. At worst, venting increases anger, spreads fear, and destroys relationships.

Consider This

Despite how much our feelings beg to be heard and validated, venting to other people is not a God-given principle. Let's consider Job, who had every reason to be distraught. His kids had just perished, all of his belongings and property had been destroyed. After a seven-day silence, Job finally began to discuss his woes with his friends. They sat there for days philosophizing about Job's issues. God finally got tired of their foolish suppositions and intervened with His majesty.

Compare Job with David. Reading David's Psalms paints the picture of a man whose feelings ran the entire gamut. Some days he was elated, yet he understood what it was like to go days on end in despair (Psalm 13:1-2). One moment he's anguished, the next he's joyous. Honestly, the first time I read the Psalms altogether, I wondered if David was stable.

Both Job and David expressed strong feelings in reaction to their respective perils. The contrast, however, lies in the audience and purpose.

First, let's consider the audience. Reckless words spoken to other people in anger and frustration are not edifying (Proverbs 12:18 and 13:3, for starters). Contrary to popular belief and practice, sitting around complaining and ruminating about our struggles does no good; it only magnifies our perception of problems, according to Dr. Michael Yapko in the book *Depression is Contagious*. Fellow human beings may comfort us with a hug or even by exposing themselves in an effort to help us know that we are not alone. But recognize that other people are not in a position to fix their own lives—let alone yours.

The purpose of venting to our God is two-fold. Sharing our deepest concerns with God contributes to our love affair with Him. When we talk to Him first about what happened at work, the kids' report cards, and the tone your mother-in-law used in a phone conversation, He reveals Himself to us as One who can relate to us on a personal level (Hebrews 4:15).

Secondly, God is the One who actually works all things together for your good (Romans 8:28). Those "little talks with Jesus" the elder saints sang about are productive. If invited, God will show up at your pity party. But it won't be long before He changes it to a praise party.

It has been my experience that after venting to God, I may not feel the need to talk to anyone else about the issue. He fills my heart with compassion for the person I'm angry with. Later, if I do decide to call a friend and share something that troubled me, I can discuss it in light of God's promises rather than an effort to gain attention for myself or momentum for my anger. At this point, I'm no longer venting but agreeing with a brother or sister to see Christ magnified.

Renew Your Mind

Whom do you contact first when you have problems—a friend or God? Is not God a close friend?

How much do feelings dictate your words or actions?

Let's be honest—it feels good to vent. Then again, many sins feel good. That said, is there any difference between responding according to feelings and responding according to flesh?

What's the difference between venting and complaining?

Remember

God is jealous for our hearts (James 4:5). He desires to respond to our deepest concerns with Himself.

Some people make cutting remarks, but the words of the wise bring healing.
Proverbs 12:18 NLT

He that keepeth his mouth keepeth his life: but he that openeth wide his lips shall have destruction.
Proverbs 13:3

This High Priest of ours understands our weaknesses, for he faced all of the same testings we do, yet he did not sin.
Hebrews 4:15 NLT

12
Stop Thinking This:
You Are Special

In the world, everyone wants to feel special. Women want their husbands to make them feel like the only woman in the world. Husbands want to be glorified and praised. Children want to be esteemed by their parents. In the world, people look to each other for validation of their special-ness. Try as they might, no human can fulfill this intrinsic need for another human. We weren't made to.

Consider This

God has carefully, precisely constructed the body of Christ for His purposes. Due to a mixing of worldly ideals and Christian beliefs, much has been preached about how some of us are called to do special things. Those who are given these "special" gifts have been blessed and highly favored of God. The rest of us...well...just be happy you're a Christian and admire the special gifts God has given to the *extra* special believers.

Ummm...nope.

You are unique, but not "special" in the sense that there's just something about you that God loves more than others just because you're...special. Recognize this as a sense of self-inflating competition that does not come from God.

The body of Christ works in unity, not competition or comparison. In Christ, no one is more special than anyone else. Whether one has been chosen to pastors tens of thousands or has been given the assignment of vacuuming a home-church, neither is more valuable than another. Actually, God has given greater honor to the parts lacking honor (1 Corinthians 12: 24). The church must be careful not to mimic the world's habit of idolizing those who are in the spotlight.

I submit to you that there will be many, many believers who will receive just as much reward as those we see celebrated in this world today. The well-known televangelists who reach millions through media will be honored as much as the men who faithfully unlocked the church doors and turned on the heat hours before the first congregants arrived in the sanctuary. Traveling preachers will learn they have nearly equal reward as the woman who ignored her arthritic fingers and baked extra pies to serve the sick and shut-in. God will only reward based on the race He marked out for each person.

This, my brothers and sisters, is what matters. This is what makes each of us a unique part of this collectively special body of Christ. Get in where God fits you in. Let's work together for His glory.

Be Renewed in Your Mind

Why do people want to feel special?

Do people feel entitled to feeling special? If so, what's causing that sense of entitlement?

If we actually believed God loved us, would we still crave people's adoration?

Remember

You are special in Christ only because *He* chose *you* to play a part in His glory. But then again, that is the case with everyone.

For the body is not one member, but many. If the foot shall say, Because I am not the hand, I am not of the body; is it therefore not of the body? And if the ear shall say, Because I am not the eye, I am not of the body; is it therefore not of the body? If the whole body were an eye, where were the hearing? If the whole were hearing, where were the smelling? But now hath God set the members every one of them in the body, as it hath pleased him.
1 Corinthians 12:14-18

13
Stop Thinking This:
Your Happiness is What Matters Most

Happiness is a sense of emotional well-being dependent upon favorable external circumstances. When times are good, people of the world are happy. Bad times bring the dumps. Neutral times bring boredom, which some believe is actually worse than the dumps. The world tells anyone who is not happy that there must be something wrong with their circumstances. They need a new job, a new spouse, new friends, a change of scenery, or even a new attitude. After all, they must do whatever it takes to make sure they stay happy.

Consider This

The problem with the believer's application of this philosophy is twofold. First, happiness flows outside-in. We have *inside-out* joy as a fruit of the Spirit (Galatians 5:22). Joy doesn't depend on circumstances, which is one reason it's incomprehensible to those who don't have it. Compared to joy, happiness is a downgrade.

Second, believers are not in a position to insist on our own happiness. Our old selves are dead in Christ. There's no one to please except Him with the life we do have. When believers make decisions on behalf of a dead man, we silence the truth that lives within us.

Still, Paul recognized that this dead man, or the flesh, still wages war with us (Romans 7:21-25). He wants his way. He screams, "I want to be happy, do what makes me feel good and feel extremely important!"

How can anything dead be so loud and so real? Well, let's imagine there's a place called OldMe, Texas. In OldMe, you put a dollar in the mailbox for the mayor every time you brushed your teeth. If you didn't, you'd be thrown in jail.

But you moved from OldMe to wherever you live now. Every time you brush your teeth, a part of you wants to pull out a dollar, but you have to remind yourself that you don't live in OldMe anymore. No matter how much the old you screams to run to the mailbox, you have to let it go. Don't feel guilty about brushing your teeth freely. It's okay. Go ahead and floss if you want to, too.

Does the law of OldMe still exist? Yes, it does— in OldMe. And if you ever went back there, you'd have to obey it, but why would you want to go back to OldMe? Really, if the city passed this silly rule, imagine the other foolishness on the books.

You've moved from OldMe. The rules of OldMe have no effect on you because you don't live there anymore. For all intents and purposes, OldMe is dead to you.

There *is* no old you to make happy. You live in our holy Christ now (Colossians 3:3). You have no lasting happiness outside of Christ. This is good news because He is constant! Believers who actually receive that revelation are emptied and free to be filled with his eternal joy.

Be Renewed in Your Mind

How long does happiness last? How long does joy last?

What's the connection between joy and peace?

What's your before-and-after Christ story? Have you shared it with anyone?

Have you actually received the revelation that you are dead?

Remember

The happiness of our old, dead selves does not matter at all. Our joy in Christ does.

But the fruit of the Spirit is love, joy, peace, longsuffering, gentleness, goodness, faith, meekness, temperance: against such there is no law.
Galatians 5:22-23

Because it is written, Be ye holy; for I am holy.
1 Peter 1:16

14
Stop Thinking This:
Take Care of Yourself First

Taking caring of yourself first means putting off everyone else's needs until after yours are met. The inherent evil trick, of course, is that when focused on yourself, your needs will never actually be met. There's always another perceived need screaming to be fulfilled before you begin to care for others.

Consider This

If the enemy can't convince us to be completely selfish, he'll do the next best thing—delay our unselfishness. When we put off a God-ordained assignment like volunteering, hosting a prayer group, or giving financially until we're in a better position, we prove that we are still trying to apply the world's rules to the Lord's system. If you haven't figured it out by now, this won't work.

The world says give when you have extra. God says you won't *have* extra until you give. We find an Old Testament example of this principle in Haggai. God wanted His people to rebuild His temple, but they decided it best to build their own fine houses first. Because of their disobedience, God said the money they earned was put "in a purse with holes in it" because He blew on what they earned (Haggai

60

1:6,9). Not until they put the kingdom of God first did the Lord bless their work (Haggai 2).

We have an even better promise in the New Testament. God's part is finished. Everything He is going to do for us has already been done through Christ. Therefore, you have already been taken care of forever in Him. The myth of the woman who wore herself out taking care of other people is not true. Actually, the woman of faith who uses her life to bless others realizes that God graces her to do more good with her life than a self-centered person could ever do.

Be Renewed in Your Mind

Why does the world mock selfless people?

What's the worst thing that could happen if you put everyone else's needs before your own?

What's the best thing that could happen if you put everyone else's needs before your own?

What does selfishness look like in your life?

Remember

Don't be afraid to spend yourself on people. Jesus spent Himself on you.

Give, and it will be given to you. A good measure, pressed down, shaken together and running over, will be poured into your lap. For with the measure you use, it will be measured to you."
Luke 6:38

15
Stop Thinking This:
Everything Happens for a Good Reason

When something inexplicable and beyond human control happens, the world will slightly concede that there is a "higher power" who pops his head into the universe every now and then. They like to think this god is on their side. They reason that if they don't deserve whatever calamity or coincidence befalls them, there has to be a good reason behind the occurrence.

So, periodically, the world winks at Him with a prayer vigil or a, "I want to thank God," during an acceptance speech. But they can't dwell on this mysterious presence too long. The thought of being at His mercy is terrifying to those who don't yet realize His love for them.

Consider This

This cliché is a half-truth, the most twisted form of deception. The first part of Romans 8:28 does say that all things work together for good, but the rest of the scripture is a qualifier. God's favorable work is only guaranteed to those who love Him and are called according to His purpose. While God Himself is good, He is not obligated to bend things toward good for people who do not love Him. Romans 8:28 comes just before Romans 8:29, where we find that the Lord uses life's circumstances (the *things* mentioned in verse 28) to conform us to the image of Christ. We may not understand the "how," but believers do know the "why." Broken hearts, joys, closed doors, and promotions all train us to be more like Christ.

But if a person has not received Christ, there is no other image for God to conform them *to*. Maybe a person of the world will be nicer, more compassionate, and less judgmental on the other side of a trial. Those things are good, and they do happen throughout the natural course of life for some who don't love God. Remember, the sun shines on the just and the unjust alike (Matthew 5:45). The difference for believers is the promise.

Recognize this rule as one of the enemy's attempts to misrepresent the truth and avoid a God-seeking, Christ-seeking panic-run in the world's system. If the world questioned the "reason" for everything, they might discover the majesty of our God and accept His love for us through Jesus.

Be Renewed in Your Mind

Is God for or against the people of the world? Does He love them?

How does this rule provide a false sense of security for unbelievers?

How can a half-truth be worse than a whole lie?

Remember

Everyone has tests. Believers have the answer key and assurance of the test's value in Christ.

And we know that all things work together for good to them that love God, to them who are the called according to his purpose. For whom he did foreknow, he also did predestinate to be conformed to the image of his Son, that he might be the firstborn among many brethren.
Romans 8:28-29

But I say to you, love your enemies, bless those who curse you, do good to those who hate you, and pray for those who spitefully use you and persecute you, that you may be sons of your Father in heaven; for He makes His sun rise on the evil and on the good, and sends rain on the just and on the unjust.
Matthew 5:44-45 NKJV

16
Stop Thinking This:
Put Family First

Absent a larger purpose, the world must devise a system of priorities. Setting the main focus on family seems honorable and right. After all, it's only natural to love the people who love you most. The Bible recognizes that most parents are good to their children (Matthew 7:8-11). By exalting family first, the enemy can appease the world's search for purpose through convincing them they've at least done *something* worthwhile.

Consider This

God has promised long life to those who honor their parents (Exodus 20:12, Ephesians 6:2-3) as well as delight and peace to parents who properly train their children (Proverbs 29:17). Neither of these rewards, however, compares to the reward of a life humbly submitted to Christ as Lord.

Putting family first actually places a great deal of undue pressure on our human relationships. When our loved ones succeed or do what we want them to do, we're elated. When they rebel or fail, we're crushed. The self-serving desire to keep ourselves happy and comfortable by controlling family members through guilt, silent treatment, "tough love," and other forms of condemnation eventually backfire. Any time we make a god of anything other than God, we will experience disappointment because people are people. Nothing more, nothing less.

Jesus commands us to love God and love people, in that order (Luke 10:27). The idea is for us to minister to our loved ones from the overflow of our love for Him. Recognizing our relationship with God through Christ frees us to love unselfishly. In Him, we can chasten our children in patience rather than exasperation, fear, or embarrassment. In His love, we trust that providing temporary shelter to in-laws who are experiencing tough times will result in opportunities to introduce them to your Source, Jehovah Jireh.

As we focus our deepest affections on Him, He has even greater impact on those within our sphere of influence. God wants to glorify their lives, too.

Be Renewed in Your Mind

How can you recognize when other people are starting to make you a little god? What is your reaction?

How does a secure relationship with God through Christ improve your relationship with people?

Can you really love people without loving God?

The Bible tells us that our heart and our treasure are strongly connected (Matthew 6:21). According to your checking or debit card account records, where is your heart?

Remember

Our eternal love affair is with the One who loved us first.

For where your treasure is, there will your heart be also.
Matthew 6:21

And he answering said, Thou shalt love the Lord thy God with all thy heart, and with all thy soul, and with all thy strength, and with all thy mind; and thy neighbour as thyself.
Luke 10:27

17
Stop Thinking This:
Experience is the Best Teacher

In the world, there are several ways people learn, including observation, training, and experiences. The lessons learned by experience seem to "stick" because they engage a person's flesh (senses) and emotions. By virtue of the fact that experience is multi-sensory, experience is a good teacher, but not the *best*. And certainly, she is not the most loving teacher.

Consider This

God uses experiences as opportunities for us to exercise our faith (James 1:2-4). However, Jesus did not ask the Father to give believers experiences to lead and guide us. He prayed for God to give us *the Holy Spirit* as our teacher (John 14:26, 1 John 2:27). God's Holy Spirit knows everything from the ordinances of heaven to how to fix a printer. He declares the end from the beginning (Isaiah 46:10). The Holy Spirit can teach you inwardly in one moment what might take fifty painful experiences and twenty years of your life for you to understand in the natural. No wonder Jesus wanted Him for us!

David recognized the word of God as the source of his wisdom. *I have more insight than all my teachers, for I meditate on your statutes. I have more understanding than the elders, for I obey your precepts* (Psalm 119:99-100). Surely, David's elders had more experience. Surely, his teachers were learned, otherwise they wouldn't have been in a position to teach him. But by meditating on the word, David was able to receive instruction straight from the Master. God doesn't just write words on a chalkboard—He writes them on our hearts! This way is better. Much better.

As believers, it is entirely possible for us to receive God's truth from the beginning and avoid unnecessary experiences that prolong our "lesson." Still, some of us rely on natural experiences to process life. A mix of the world's system and God's system might look like this in the life of a believer:

1. Read or hear a Word from the Lord.

2. Resist the Word (sin) and yield to reason/flesh.

3. As a result of rebellion, undergo an experience that teaches the same lesson expressed in step 1.

4. Review and meditate on the Word.

5. Repent and ask the Lord to fix whatever got messed up in step 3.

6. Thank God that you have finally received the Word.

Do we really need steps 2, 3, and 5? As my

grandmother would say, "You ain't even gotta go through all that."

If we receive His instruction and take His Word for the tried-and-true, age-old wisdom that it *is*, we don't have to bare the scars of disobedience. Then, perhaps our testimony won't be that God continually rescues us, but that He *keeps* us by His word.

Be Renewed in Your Mind

Why would the enemy want people to go through harsh experiences? What is his goal through these experiences?

Does our loving God also allow His people to go through harsh experiences? Why or why not?

What has the Holy Spirit directly taught you? How long did it take for you to "get" what He taught you?

Remember

Experience is not the best teacher; the Holy Spirit is.

And I will put my spirit within you, and cause you to walk in my statutes, and ye shall keep my judgments, and do them.
Ezekiel 36:27

But the Comforter, which is the Holy Ghost, whom the Father will send in my name, he shall teach you all things, and bring all things to your remembrance, whatsoever I have said unto you.
John 14:26

My brethren, count it all joy when ye fall into divers temptations; Knowing this, that the trying of your faith worketh patience. But let patience have her perfect work, that ye may be perfect and entire, wanting nothing.
James 1:2-4

18
Stop Thinking This:
We're on a Quest for Wholeness

The world invests a great deal of its resources in the pursuit of wholeness. The enemy displays an illusion of wholeness through self-help gurus, "spiritual" advisors, and others who claim to have achieved wholeness apart from God—or maybe with God (a.k.a. "the universe") on their side.

Unfortunately, "whole" unbelievers will still be eternally separated from the love of God.

The Believers' Uncommon Sense

If you haven't figured it out already, we have to be on alert for the catch phrases of our time. Words like "wholeness" and "empowerment" are tossed around in churches, secular groups, cults, and new-age groups alike. Make no mistake: The enemy's attempt to portray life's purpose as generic and applicable to everyone is actually his clever plan to exclude the name above every name—Jesus. The enemy is fine with folks searching for wholeness, balance, and accountability. He's even fine with people believing in some kind of God because the world isn't Anti-God so much as it is Anti-*Christ*.

When preachers and ministers attempt to make the Word more palatable or dress it up in a worldly package, we actually hide the power of the gospel behind our own clever schemes. We reason that people aren't ready for the truth of salvation, the Bible bores them, and so we need funny little analogies to keep people from falling asleep in the pews. The irony in all this is that the gospel of Christ preached *is* the power unto salvation (Romans 1:16). The reason more people aren't enamored with Christ is because He's nowhere to be heard or seen in a great number of messages preached. When the goal is wholeness rather than holiness or accountability groups versus the righteous conviction of the indwelling Holy Spirit, we remove Christ from the equation, leaving us only to ourselves and whatever self-manufactured strength we can conjure up.

Another message of the wholeness quest is that if you work out or through all your issues (physically, emotionally, financially, etc.), then and only then will you be okay. There are several reasons why this principle is inconsistent with God's plan for believers.

1) Spiritual issues aren't eligible to be "worked" out by man-made remedies. Deliverance is promised in Christ and received by faith, the same way you received salvation. It may help to talk with others along the way, but the words of encouragement and the testimonies they share will only take permanent root if you receive them in faith. But don't worry! You have the faith *of* Christ (Galatians 2:20,

KJV). Yes—He has given us His faith. Receive it!

2) We already *are* okay in Christ. Here again is the classic forbidden-fruit-scheme, trying to tempt us against God.

3) While we can expect to live a full, abundant life in Christ, we still have an enemy in the land. Until he is confined to hell forever, we have been given the power to keep him in check (Luke 10:19). We are not free from his whisperings or his *attempts* to overtake us. Again, don't be alarmed by this truth. The point of God allowing us to endure trials is not to have us wounded, but to give us practice in wielding the Sword. Go to any T-ball game and you'll notice that father's like to see their children win!

4) This is not our home. Even during the times when everything appears to be going smoothly, the Spirit within still longs for our heavenly dwelling and cannot be satisfied in this foreign land. Our most whole state will be revealed when Christ returns and we are changed permanently and completely disconnected from this pestering flesh (Colossians 3:3-4).

You have the fullness of Christ and His holiness dwelling within you right now. Don't let the enemy set you off on another wild goose chase for something you already have in Christ.

Be Renewed in Your Mind

Why is the word "wholeness" more acceptable than "holiness" in the world? In churches?

Do you consider yourself holy? Why or why not? What does God consider you?

Why are believers sometimes intimidated by their own holiness?

Can one actually be whole outside of Christ?

Remember

For believers, our holiness *is* our present-tense wholeness.

For I am not ashamed of the gospel of Christ: for it is the power of God unto salvation to every one that believeth; to the Jew first, and also to the Greek.
Romans 1:16

You see, we don't go around preaching about ourselves. We preach that Jesus Christ is Lord, and we ourselves are your servants for Jesus' sake.
2 Corinthians 4:5 NLT

19
Stop Thinking This:
Keep an Open Mind

Those who have not yet received Jesus as Lord and Savior are still searching for the truth. Indeed, *they* need to keep an open mind so they can receive Him. Believers are not in the same position.

Consider This

The idea of an open-minded person implies one who is flexible and recognizes there is more than one "right" way to do or view things. Contrarily, those with closed minds are viewed as ignorant, uncultured, or even arrogant. Perhaps it is advisable to keep an open mind when it comes to matters of taste and preference. But what applies to fashion or food does not apply to our faith.

Once Christ has revealed Himself to you and you have accepted Him as savior, there is no need for you to open your mind to false doctrines or worldly ideals. In fact, God recognized the need for us to be sealed in the Holy Spirit (Ephesians 1:13). He has preserved us for Himself.

The enemy would have us believe that we're missing out on something by intentionally closing our minds to the world's ways. When we don't live by the evening news, accept an invitation to a universal spirituality conference, or opt out of watching a questionable movie with friends, he whispers that we're primitive, unsophisticated. Once again, he's using the old forbidden-fruit-and-tree trick. He's attempting to convince us that in order to be a well-rounded, intelligent person, we need to keep our minds open to many different interpretations, paths to happiness, and ways of thinking. What a lie!

We close our minds not because we're childish or even afraid of a challenge to our faith. Rather, the consecrated mind does not seek or give room to corruption.

God's plan is not to keep us ignorant, but to teach us His way because it's the *best* way. His heart is good. His ways are good. There is joy, love, and fearlessness in His way. Just as believers don't want open marriages, God's not interested in open covenants.

Jesus commanded the disciples to be wise as serpents, yet innocent as doves (Matthew 10:16). Ask the Holy Spirit to show you only what leads to Christ's glory in your life. Resist the urge to be your own god, and stand guard against false teachings and distractions (i.e., "open doors") intended to lead you astray.

Be Renewed in Your Mind

Is God's heart toward us really good? If we actually

believe this, how are we so easily tempted to stray from His way? If not, what has He done (or not done) that will not contribute to eternal joy for you 100 years from now?

How do you view people who have completely sold out to Christ? Are you afraid of them? Are they weird? Are you one of "them"? If not, do you want to be? What does God want you to be?

Our omnipresent, omniscient God has seen all manner of sin, but He has never sinned. What's the difference between being aware of sin and opening your mind/heart to sin?

Why was the knowledge of both good an evil such a temptation for Eve? Did God ever intend for us to know evil?

Remember

You have the mind of Christ (1 Corinthians 2:16). He understands the ways of the world, but He does not operate by them. Neither do we.

In whom [Christ] ye also trusted, after that ye heard the word of truth, the gospel of your salvation: in whom also after that ye believed, ye were sealed with that holy Spirit of promise, Which is the earnest of our inheritance until the redemption of the purchased

possession, unto the praise of his glory.
Ephesians 1:13-14, brackets added

Behold, I send you forth as sheep in the midst of wolves: be ye therefore wise as serpents, and harmless as doves.
Matthew 10:16

20
Stop Thinking This:
The Bible is a Practical Book of Principles

Because God's ways are good, the ideals of our faith, the teachings of Christ, and the wisdom of the Word may lead to a fairly good life even for those who do not believe in Christ as Savior. In fact, many of the world's religions can be summed up with the golden rule: Treat others the way you want to be treated.

As long as people view the Bible as a document with generic guidelines, the enemy can lull them into a sense of their own goodness apart from Christ. In fact, much of the world lives in this man-made bubble of universal relative *okay*-ness that does not overtly contradict biblical principles. This seems good and right.

Unfortunately, there is a way that *seems* right, but leads to death (Proverbs 14:12).

Consider This

The adjective "practical" implies a sense that something is doable. Realistic. Capable of being to accomplish with your own hands by following a formula in your own strength. With this definition in mind, there is absolutely nothing practical about the gift of Christ. Really, in the beginning was God?

Nothing was here before Him—how is that even possible? Then a snake talked a woman into sin? Centuries later, a virgin gets pregnant? God comes to earth as the son of man? This man dies on a cross and forgives sins you and I haven't even committed yet? And we're going to live with him eternally? Can you even wrap your mind around the concept of eternity? For real?

Let's be honest with each other and with the world: There's something completely impractical, yet totally true about life in Christ. One can "apply" the principles of Christianity and, in all probability, walk through a decent life. But there is something more. Something that escapes those who don't believe.

That "something" is Christ. He is supernatural. He is the mystery revealed to believers (Colossians 1:27), the power of the Bible hidden from the world. He is the Word living within.

He cannot be reduced to practical means.

Be Renewed in Your Mind

Why does Christ make all the difference?

How does being good mask the need for Christ?

Read John 10:17-27. Can a person actually be good without Christ?

Remember

Don't reduce spirituality to practicality.

Whereof I am made a minister, according to the
dispensation of God which is given to me for you, to
fulfil the word of God; Even the mystery which hath
been hid from ages and from generations, but now is
made manifest to his saints: To whom God would
make known what is the riches of the glory of this
mystery among the Gentiles; which is Christ in you,
the hope of glory...
Colossians 1:25-27

21
Stop Thinking This:
Balance Your Christian Life with your Real Life

If the enemy cannot get religious people to reject Christ entirely, the best he can do is attempt to reduce Christ. By convincing people to compartmentalize life's roles into two separate categories (self-directed and God-directed), the enemy authors havoc through double-mindedness.

Consider This

The Bible does not instruct believers to make distinctions between who we are in Christ and who we are in real life. Everything we do, from mowing the lawn to voting in an election to teaching a Bible study class, flows from the life of Christ within us. He doesn't turn off and on like a light switch—He *is* the light.

Here is what we have to know as believers: When Christ died on the cross, we died *with* Him. When He rose, we rose *in* Him. If it were possible that Christ could somehow cease to exist, we would also cease to exist because we cannot do anything apart from Him. For those who have exchanged their lives for Christ, there is no other life available to us now. There is nothing to balance. "I am crucified with Christ:

nevertheless I live; yet not I, but Christ liveth in me…" Galatians 2:20.

The beauty of Christ alive in us is that we don't have to *try* to be like Him. You are in Christ and He is in you. Sounds difficult, but we have already established that the things of God are supernatural. Don't try to boil it down to putting on a glove or some kind of pretzel analogy. God's ways are not like anything you know. Life in Him is not like anything you've imagined, so don't waste your time with intellectualism. Go there by faith, which is how you live your entire life in Christ.

Be Renewed in Your Mind

Under what circumstances, if any, should believers put God's agenda aside and work toward the common good of everyone?

Christ warned the Laodicea against being lukewarm (Revelations 3:14-22). What was his biggest concern for them? What was the remedy?

Where do double-minded people draw the line when it comes to Christianity? Money?
Politics? Career? Their children's safety?

When we attempt to keep some areas under our own control, what does that say about our faith in God's love and His word?

Remember

Your life in Christ *is* your real life.

*Now the just shall live by faith: but if any man draw
back, my soul shall have no pleasure in him.*
Hebrews 10:38

Resources

Below is a list of books and resources I highly recommend as God carries out His commitment to transform you into Christ's image. I am grateful to have been a part of your journey, and I look forward to our glorious eternity together in His presence!

Books

52 Lies Heard in Church Every Sunday (Steve McVey)

Christian Atheist: Believing in God but Living as if He Doesn't Exist (Greg Groeschel)

* *Driven by Eternity* (John Bevere)

* *Gracewalk* (Steve McVey)

Lies Women Believe and the Truth that Sets Them Free (Nancy Leigh DeMoss)

The Sacred Romance (Brent Curtis and John Eldredge)

* Compare the authors' contrasting points in these two books with scripture.

Digital Resources

Biblegateway.com – research scriptures in various translations (also available as an app)

Blueletterbible.org – research the original language of the scriptures (also available as an app for Apple devices)

Daily Audio Bible – travel through the Bible in a year. Each year, listen to a new translation.

Other Books by Michelle Stimpson

Non-Fiction

Married for Five Minutes - Take a 5-minute peek inside real marriages facing challenges that threaten to blur the reflection of Christ that marriage was created to be.

War Room Strategies – A step-by-step guide to developing effectual prayers for God's Glory

Fiction

Deacon Brown's Daughters - Stanley Brown's got a lot of cleaning up to do if he wants to become a deacon…and it starts with his children.

Mama B: A Time to Speak –The good folks at Mt. Zion Baptist are doing their best to keep the church going while Pastor takes time off, but Mama B can only take so much of the interim minister's foolishness!

Stuck on You - Braxton Stoneworth and Tiffany Warren were just friends in college...until one spring night when the love bug bit. But Braxton threw it all away to join his fraternity. Will Tiffany forgive him ten years later?

Boaz Brown – When LaShondra Smith prayed for the right man, she forgot to specify his race. Can she see past the wrapping paper to receive the gift?

No Weapon Formed – Revisit LaShondra and Stelson ten years after their whirlwind romance. Now married and the parents of two bi-racial children, they must learn to toggle faith and clashing cultures.

The Blended Blessings Series –Angelia didn't get it right with her first marriage. Or her second. She hopes this third time will work out, but with twin step-daughters and a mother-in-law who don't like the status quo, this may be the most difficult marriage yet.

A Forgotten Love – One bad play brought London Whitfield's brief professional football career to a devastating end. Back at home and reluctantly living life as an average Joe, London reconnects with the one girl, Daphne, who represents the best and the worst relationship he ever experienced.

All This Love - Knox Stoneworth got dumped at the altar—literally—and has spent the last few years burying himself in work to move past the pain. After a night of celebrating his parents' anniversary, Knox meets a stranger who just might change his mind about his future.

What About Momma's House? - Katrice, Montrel and Junior are siblings who couldn't be more different, but they all have one thing in common: plans for Momma's house.

About the Author

Michelle Stimpson's works include the highly acclaimed *Boaz Brown*, *Divas of Damascus Road* (National Bestseller), and *Falling Into Grace,* which has been optioned for a movie. She has published several short stories for high school students through her educational publishing company at WeGottaRead.com.

Michelle serves in women's ministry at Oak Cliff Bible Fellowship in Dallas, TX. She regularly speaks at special events and writing workshops sponsored by churches, schools, book clubs, and educational organizations.

The Stimpsons are proud parents of two young adults, grandparents of one super-sweet granddaughter, and the owners of one Cocker Spaniel, Mimi, who loves to watch televangelists.

Visit Michelle online:
www.MichelleStimpson.com
https://www.facebook.com/MichelleStimpsonWrites